THE POWER
OF
PRESSURE

ANDREW DUNN
Illustrated by
ED CARR

Wayland

Titles in this series
Heat
It's Electric
Lifting by Levers
The Power of Pressure
Simple Slopes
Wheels at Work

First published in 1992 by
Wayland (Publishers) Ltd
61 Western Road, Hove
East Sussex, BN3 1JD, England

Editor: Anna Girling
Design: Carr Associates Graphics, Brighton

British Library Cataloguing in Publication Data
Dunn, Andrew
  The power of pressure.–(How things work)
  I. Title   II. Series
  372.3

HARDBACK ISBN 0-7502-0226-2

PAPERBACK ISBN 0-7502-0956-9

Typeset by Dorchester Typesetting Group Ltd
Printed in Italy by G. Canale & C.S.p.A. Turin

Contents

Words in *italic* in the text are explained in the glossary on page 30.

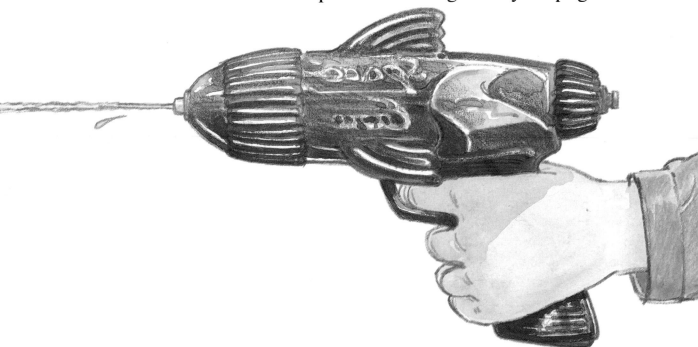

The force in fluids

Machines, whether as simple as a bottle opener or as complicated as a space rocket, all need effort, or force, to do their jobs. Some machines take this force from the power of human muscles, or from electricity. But some machines use the pressure of fluids.

Pressure is all around us. It is any force pressing on a surface. A fluid is anything that can flow – a gas, such as air, or a liquid, such as water. All fluids push on the things around them with pressure.

The tiny *particles* of gases are moving all the time, bumping into each other and any surface they hit. The air around us has pressure – because of this constant movement, and also because of the enormous weight of all the air above us.

In liquids, the particles do not move as much as in gases, so pressure is mostly caused by the liquid's own weight, or by something trying to squash it.

This scene looks calm, but the tiny particles in the air and water are moving all the time.

4

How much pressure?

Air pressure is bigger than you might think. Try this experiment (over a sink, just in case!).

Fill a glass or cup to the brim with water. Cover it completely with a piece of card. Now, holding the card in place, turn the glass upside-down . . . and let go of the card. What happens?

Air pressure holds the water in. It presses up on the card with far more force than the weight of the water pushing down.

Luckily the pressure of the fluids inside our bodies just about *balances* the air pressure outside, or we would be squashed flat!

Some pressure machines

Machines use pressure in many different ways. Some machines use liquids, like oil or water. Others use gases, such as *carbon dioxide*. Most use air pressure. Some pressure machines blow or spray, and some suck. Can you see which of these machines blow and which suck?

Drinking straw

Hovercraft

6

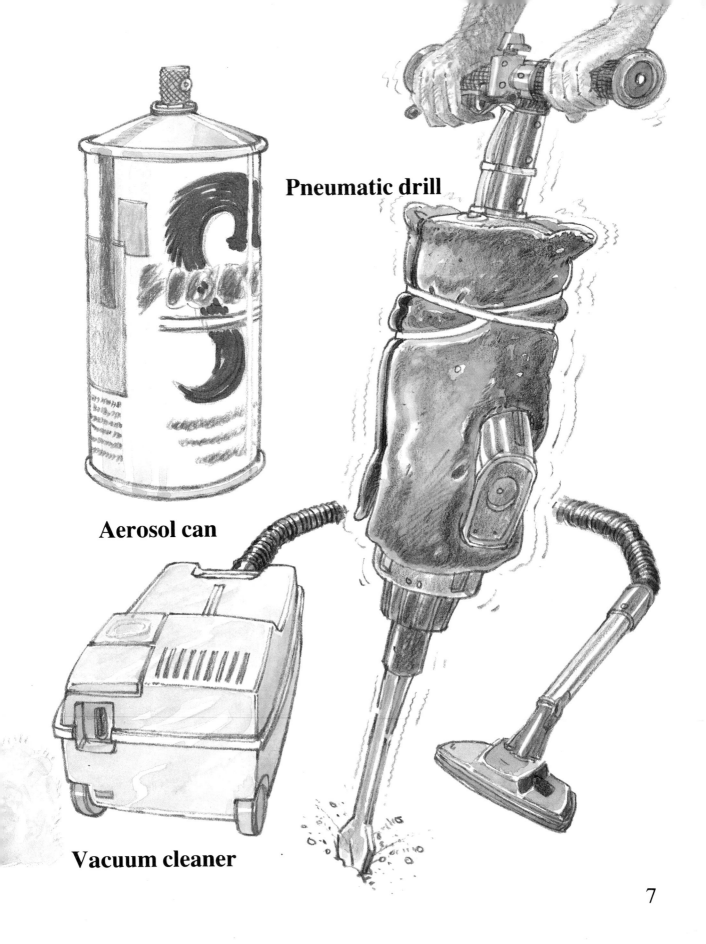

Pneumatic drill

Aerosol can

Vacuum cleaner

The principle of pressure

You can increase pressure in any fluid by squeezing lots of it into a small space. You can also lower its pressure, by giving it more room. But nature likes things to balance each other. The principle of all pressure machines is this: any fluid will move, if it can, until it has the same pressure as its surroundings.

You can squash air into a balloon by blowing into it. But when you let go, air will rush out. It will keep coming out until the air inside has the same pressure as the air outside.

A balloon stays blown up if no air can escape. But when you let it go the extra air rushes out.

8

Strong pressure

Pressure can be a very strong force.
Normally, because air is spread
evenly all around us, and because
our bodies are full of blood and
water at about the same
pressure, we do not notice
air pressure. You only have
to take some air out of one
place, though, or put it into
another, and the balance will
have gone. Then you will
suddenly notice the effects
of pressure.

Pressure pumps

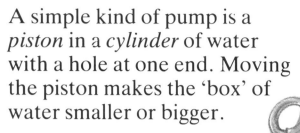

A simple kind of pump is a *piston* in a *cylinder* of water with a hole at one end. Moving the piston makes the 'box' of water smaller or bigger.

When the 'box' is made smaller, the water pressure goes up. The water will try to escape the only way it can – through the hole – in a powerful jet of water.

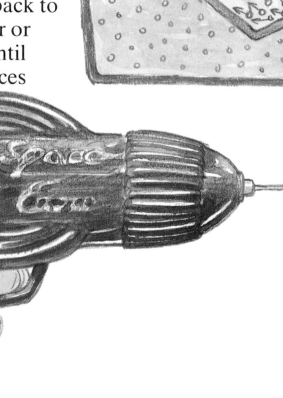

When the piston moves back to make the 'box' bigger, air or water will be sucked in until the pressure inside balances the pressure outside.

Valves

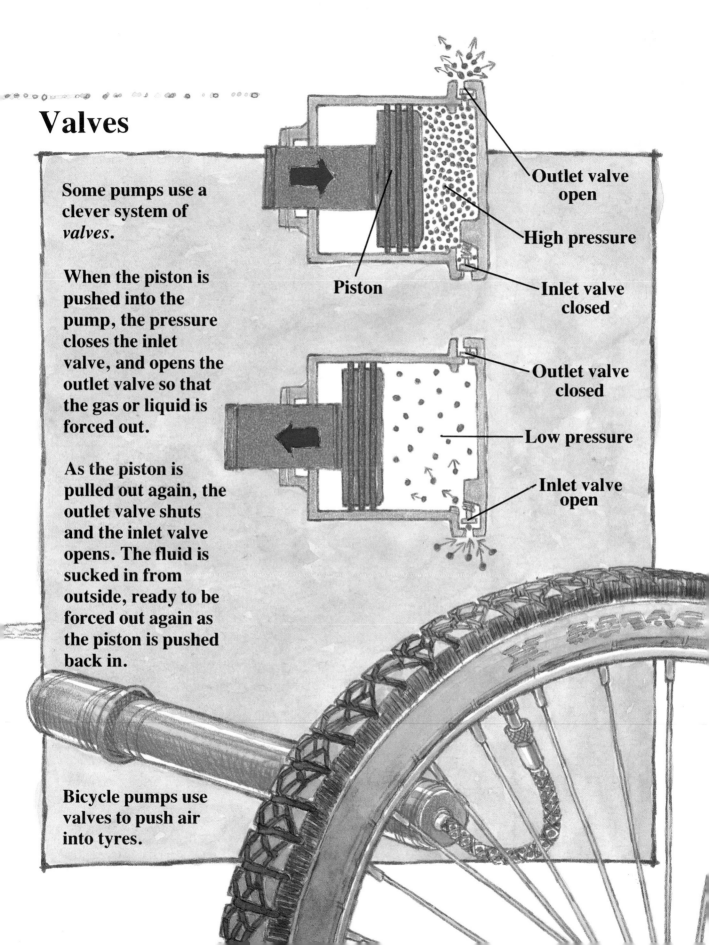

Some pumps use a clever system of *valves*.

When the piston is pushed into the pump, the pressure closes the inlet valve, and opens the outlet valve so that the gas or liquid is forced out.

As the piston is pulled out again, the outlet valve shuts and the inlet valve opens. The fluid is sucked in from outside, ready to be forced out again as the piston is pushed back in.

Bicycle pumps use valves to push air into tyres.

Outlet valve open

High pressure

Piston

Inlet valve closed

Outlet valve closed

Low pressure

Inlet valve open

More pumps

The piston pump and bicycle pump both have a part – a piston – which moves back and forth to increase the pressure on the fluid.

Other pumps use a circular, or rotary, movement to raise pressure. These pumps work in different ways, but they are all useful in that they can produce a steady stream of pressurized fluid.

Rotary pumps are used in car engines and petrol pumps.

Petrol stations use rotary pumps. The petrol is pulled up from big tanks underground.

Cooling system

Car engines need to be cooled by a steady flow of water. The water is pushed round the engine by a rotary pump.

The round pump contains *blades* that spin round. The water enters at the centre of the pump and the revolving blades swirl it round, flinging it outwards.

It leaves through an outlet in the wall of the pump at high pressure.

The water is pushed through the engine and becomes hot.

It then goes through the car's radiator where it is cooled, ready to be pumped round the engine again.

Pneumatic machines

Pneumatic machines use air pressure. The pneumatic tyre, for example, simply contains air at high pressure, providing an air 'cushion' between the wheel and the ground. This evens out the bumps and makes for a smoother journey.

Hovercraft

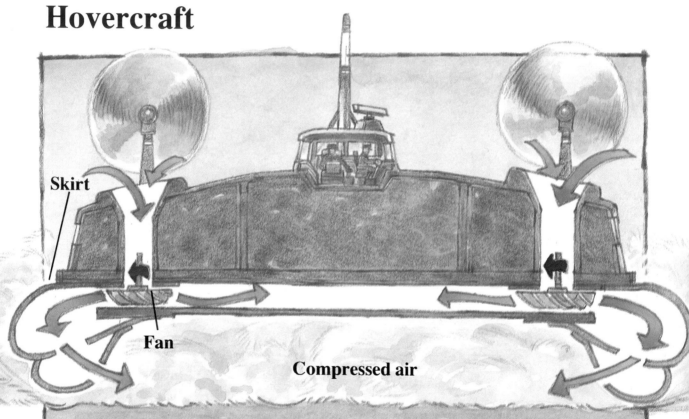

Skirt

Fan

Compressed air

A hovercraft rides on a cushion of air.

Air is sucked in and *compressed* by big fans inside the hovercraft, giving it enough force to lift the craft and its passengers.

The air is held in under the hovercraft by a thick 'skirt' made of rubber.

The hovercraft floats above the surface of the ground or sea, without causing *friction*. Normal propellers push it along.

Pneumatic drill

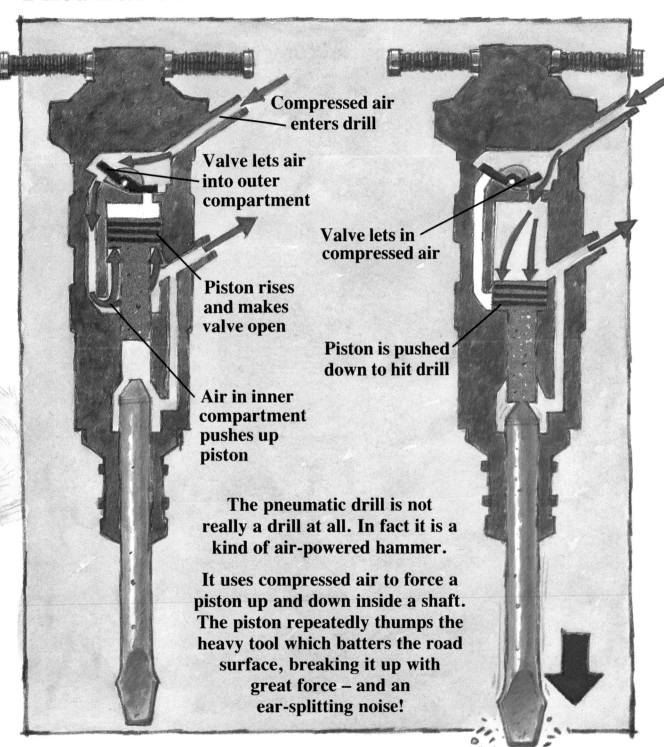

Compressed air enters drill

Valve lets air into outer compartment

Valve lets in compressed air

Piston rises and makes valve open

Piston is pushed down to hit drill

Air in inner compartment pushes up piston

The pneumatic drill is not really a drill at all. In fact it is a kind of air-powered hammer.

It uses compressed air to force a piston up and down inside a shaft. The piston repeatedly thumps the heavy tool which batters the road surface, breaking it up with great force – and an ear-splitting noise!

Hydraulic machines

Car brakes

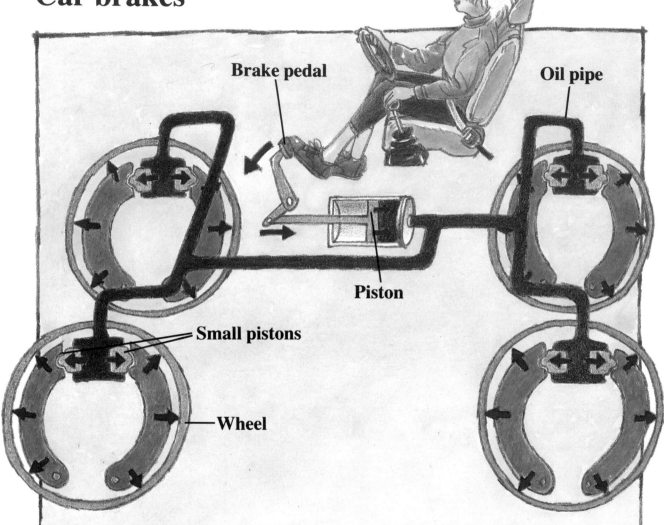

Brake pedal

Oil pipe

Piston

Small pistons

Wheel

Car brakes are *hydraulic* machines. The word hydraulic means they use the pressure in liquids.

The brake pedal pushes down a piston in a cylinder which is connected by pipes to smaller cylinders, also with pistons, next to the wheels.

The whole system is filled with oil. The oil does not 'squash' much, so pushing on the main piston raises the pressure all through the system.

The pressure pushes the smaller pistons out so that they rub against the wheels, and friction slows down the car.

Car lift

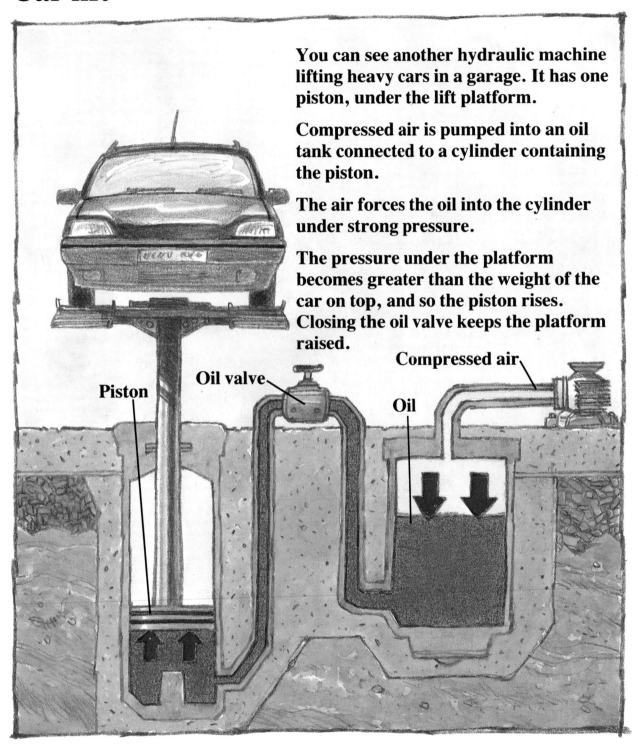

You can see another hydraulic machine lifting heavy cars in a garage. It has one piston, under the lift platform.

Compressed air is pumped into an oil tank connected to a cylinder containing the piston.

The air forces the oil into the cylinder under strong pressure.

The pressure under the platform becomes greater than the weight of the car on top, and so the piston rises. Closing the oil valve keeps the platform raised.

Compressed air

Oil valve

Oil

Piston

Sprays and jets

When a liquid is forced through a small hole by pressure, it forms a powerful jet. This jet usually breaks up into a spray of tiny droplets in the air.

The *nozzle* of an *aerosol* spray can is so tiny that the spray becomes a fine mist. Many liquid products, such as hair sprays and fly killers, work better as a spray.

Dishwasher

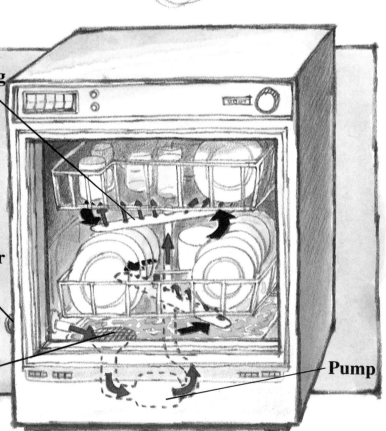

Dishwashers produce pressure using rotary pumps.

Hot soapy water is forced around pipes and into spraying arms which spin round above and below the dishes.

The water is flung out of nozzles in the arms, spraying the dishes clean.

Spraying arm

Water inlet

Filter

Pump

Aerosol can

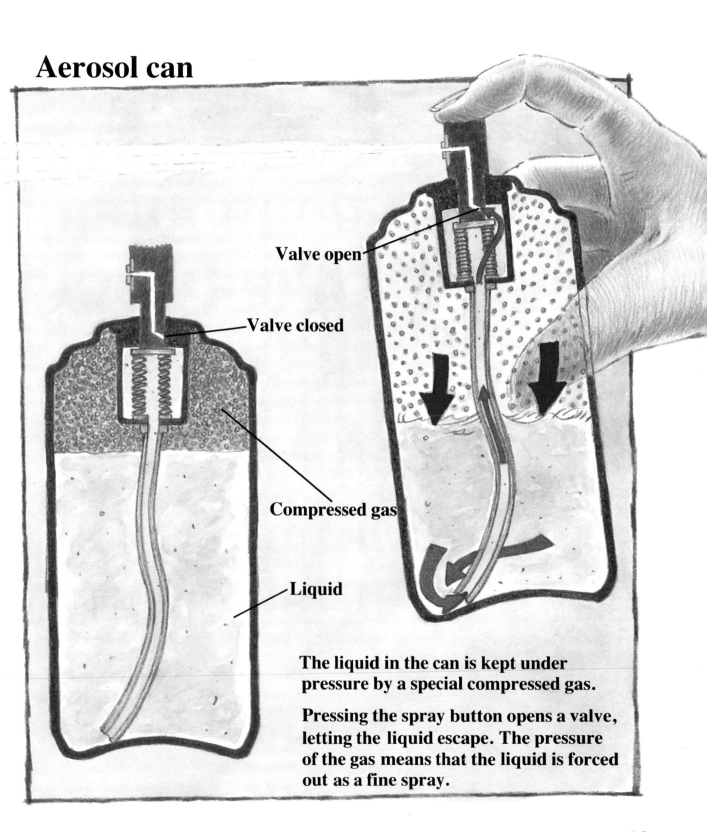

Valve open

Valve closed

Compressed gas

Liquid

The liquid in the can is kept under pressure by a special compressed gas.

Pressing the spray button opens a valve, letting the liquid escape. The pressure of the gas means that the liquid is forced out as a fine spray.

Sucking machines

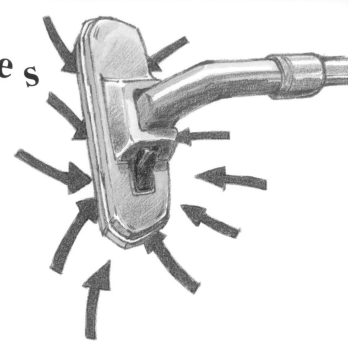

Most machines which work by pressure use extra pressure to blow or force something outwards. But the balance can also be upset the other way, by removing pressure. Removing pressure causes *suction*.

When you drink through a straw, you start by sucking the air out of it. This means that there is no air pressing down on the drink inside the straw.

But air is still pressing down on the drink in the cup, and that forces the drink up the straw, into your mouth.

When you stop sucking, the air pressure at each end of the straw is equal. So the milk slips down again.

Vacuum cleaner

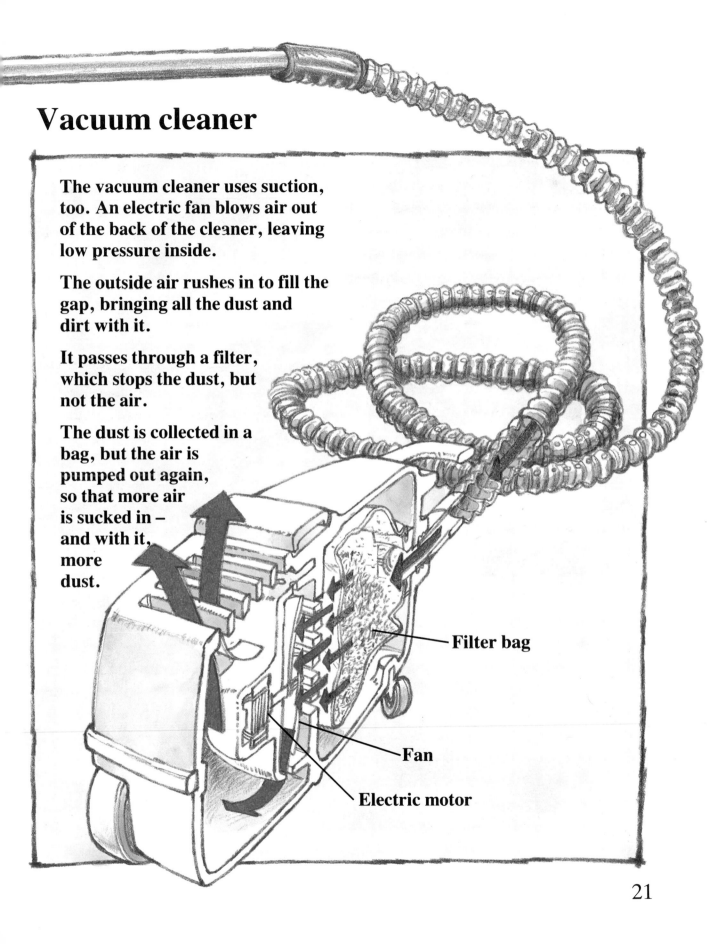

The vacuum cleaner uses suction, too. An electric fan blows air out of the back of the cleaner, leaving low pressure inside.

The outside air rushes in to fill the gap, bringing all the dust and dirt with it.

It passes through a filter, which stops the dust, but not the air.

The dust is collected in a bag, but the air is pumped out again, so that more air is sucked in – and with it, more dust.

Filter bag

Fan

Electric motor

The siphon

In a siphon, pressure makes water flow uphill! You can make a siphon with a piece of plastic or rubber tubing. You can buy this from a model shop.

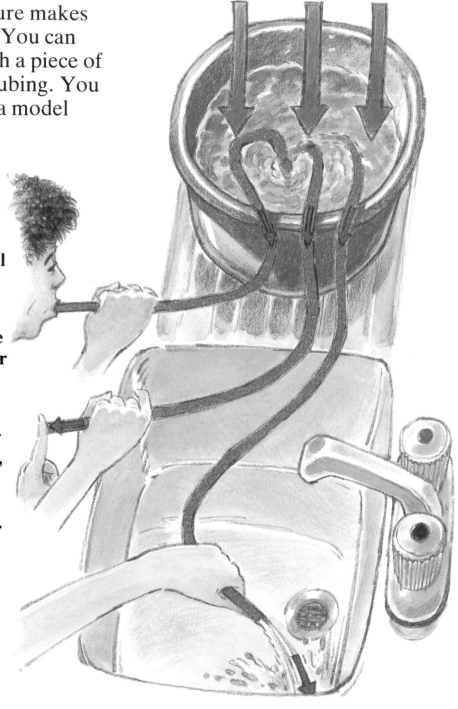

Air pressure

Put one end of the tubing into a bowl of water and suck at the other end until the tube is full of water.

Put a finger over this end to hold the water in, and lower it into the sink.

As long as this end of the tube is lower than the other end, water will flow up from the bowl and down into the sink.

The weight of the water in the tube makes the siphon start flowing, and air pressure on the water in the bowl does the rest.

Toilet cistern

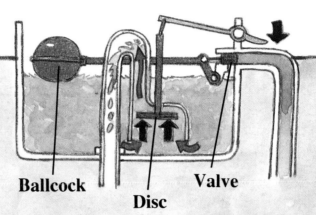

Ballcock **Disc** **Valve**

Many toilets flush using a siphon. A tube goes up from the *cistern* and down into the toilet bowl.

1 Disc raises water to start siphon.

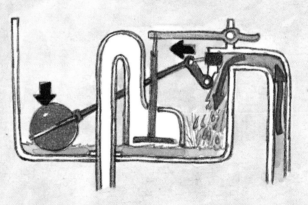

When the handle is pushed down, it pulls up a disc which takes water up with it and starts the siphon flowing. It only stops when the cistern is almost empty.

2 Weight of water in pipe keeps siphon flowing.

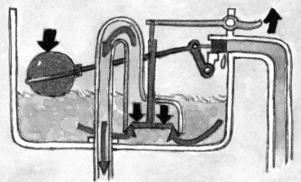

By then the floating *ballcock* has fallen far enough to open a valve which allows the cistern to refill.

3 Cistern empties and siphon is broken. Lowered ballcock opens valve.

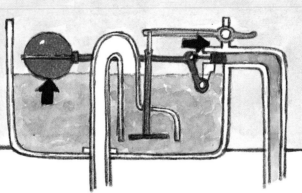

The siphon is now full of air, and nothing will happen until the handle is pressed down again.

4 Cistern refills and valve closes.

23

Experiments with pressure

Here are some pressure tricks you can surprise your friends with!

The obedient shower

Use a corkscrew to make a few holes in the base of an empty washing-up liquid bottle.

Put the bottle in a bowl of water and squeeze out all the air.

Before you take the bottle out of the water, place your finger over the hole in the nozzle at the top.

When you take the bottle out, lift your finger and the shower will start. Cover the hole again, and it will stop.

The water can only fall from the bottom when air can get into the top. This is because the pressure is the same top and bottom. Otherwise, the air pressure underneath holds it in.

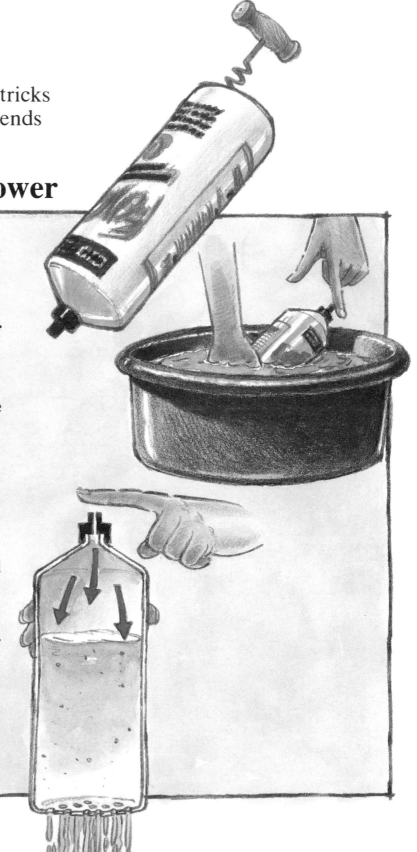

The spouting fountain

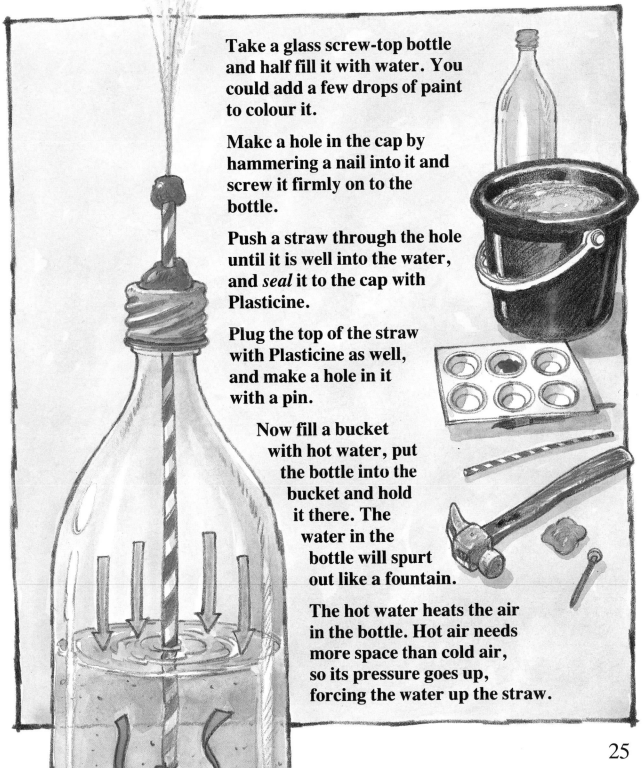

Take a glass screw-top bottle and half fill it with water. You could add a few drops of paint to colour it.

Make a hole in the cap by hammering a nail into it and screw it firmly on to the bottle.

Push a straw through the hole until it is well into the water, and *seal* it to the cap with Plasticine.

Plug the top of the straw with Plasticine as well, and make a hole in it with a pin.

Now fill a bucket with hot water, put the bottle into the bucket and hold it there. The water in the bottle will spurt out like a fountain.

The hot water heats the air in the bottle. Hot air needs more space than cold air, so its pressure goes up, forcing the water up the straw.

25

Air pressure and flight

Try these experiments to find out how air pressure is used to make an aeroplane fly.

Hold a sheet of paper by two corners so that one edge touches your bottom lip and the sheet hangs down. Now blow hard over it. What happens?

Now hold two sheets so that they hang down with a small gap between them. What do you expect will happen when you blow into the gap? Try it. Is that what you expected to happen?

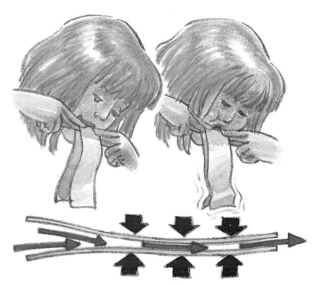

You have just shown yourself the principle of flight. What happens is that when air moves at speed, its pressure drops. So when you blow between the pieces of paper, the pressure there is lower than outside. The greater pressure on the outside of the sheets pushes them together. The wings of aeroplanes are designed in a special way to make use of this principle.

This aircraft wing is folded. The top is rounded and the bottom is flat.

Wings

An aeroplane wing is shaped so that the air on top has to travel further than the air underneath.

This makes the air on top travel faster, so its pressure drops.

The greater air pressure below lifts the wing, and the aeroplane. This is how huge modern aircraft stay up in the sky.

The power of pressure

The air around us at ground level presses on everything with a pressure, or force, of about one kilogram on every square centimetre. Deep in the oceans, thousands of metres down, the pressure of water is measured in hundreds of *tonnes* pressing on each square centimetre. But people still go there, in submarines carefully designed so that they are not crushed by the enormous forces.

Left *Water pressure gets higher the deeper you dive. This swimmer has to breathe air at higher pressure than normal to keep her lungs working.*

Right Astronauts no longer need to wear heavy space suits. These astronauts are on board the American Space Shuttle. Inside, scientists have been able to create the right pressure and conditions for humans to live.

People have learned to live in space too, high above the edge of the *atmosphere*, where there is almost no pressure at all. They have done this by creating an *artificial* atmosphere at normal pressure.

Here on earth, people have learned to use the power of pressure to make anything from the vacuum cleaner to the hydraulic lift in the car workshop. By understanding its principles, people can use pressure to apply just the right amount of force exactly where they want it.

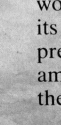

Glossary

Aerosol   A fine mist made of tiny droplets of liquid in the air.

Artificial   Made or created by people, rather than happening naturally.

Atmosphere   The layer of air that surrounds the earth. It is thickest at ground level and becomes thinner the higher you go. In space, there is no air at all.

Balance   Two objects balance each other when they press with the same force, or when they weigh the same as each other.

Ballcock   A device for controlling water coming into a toilet cistern. A ball floating in the cistern is connected to a valve. When the toilet is flushed, the ball falls and the valve opens, letting in fresh water.

Blades   In a rotary pump, the flat parts of the propeller which spin round.

Carbon dioxide   A colourless gas which is part of the air we breathe.

Cistern   The water tank above a toilet which also contains the flushing mechanism.

Compressed   Something is compressed when it is squashed so that it takes up less space than it would normally.

Cylinder   A round, hollow tube, like a length of drain-pipe.

Friction   The force that makes it hard to push an object across a surface, because the two things rub against each other.

Hydraulic   A machine is hydraulic if it works by using the pressure in a liquid, rather than a gas.

Nozzle   A small opening at the end of a pipe or tube.

Particles   The smallest specks of a substance.

Piston   A round plate of metal which fits inside a tube. It is attached to a rod, and the rod and piston move up and down in the tube.

Pneumatic   A machine is pneumatic if it works by using the pressure in air or other gases.

Seal   To close tightly so that no air or water can escape.

Suction   The force produced by making something have less pressure instead of more – in other words, by sucking instead of blowing.

Tonne   A thousand kilograms.

Valves   Clever devices for controlling the flow of a liquid or gas. A valve opens rather like a door to let the fluid go through an opening, and closes to stop it.

Books to read

For younger readers:
Air in Action by Robin Kerrod
(Cherrytree Books, 1988)
Flight by Malcolm Dixon
(Wayland, 1990)
Young Engineer in the Air by
Graham Weston (Wayland, 1983)

For older readers:
How Things Work by Steve Parker
(Kingfisher, 1990)
The Way Things Work by David
Macaulay (Dorling Kindersley,
1988)
The World of Machines (Can You
Believe It? series) by Jenny
Vaughan (Cherrytree Books, 1990)

Index

Picture acknowledgements

The publishers would like to thank the following for providing the photographs for this book: Cephas Picture Library 12 (Stuart Boreham); NASA/Science Photo Library 29; Sefton Photo Library 26; Tony Stone Worldwide 28 (Chris Harvey); Wayland Picture Library 20; Zefa 4, 8.